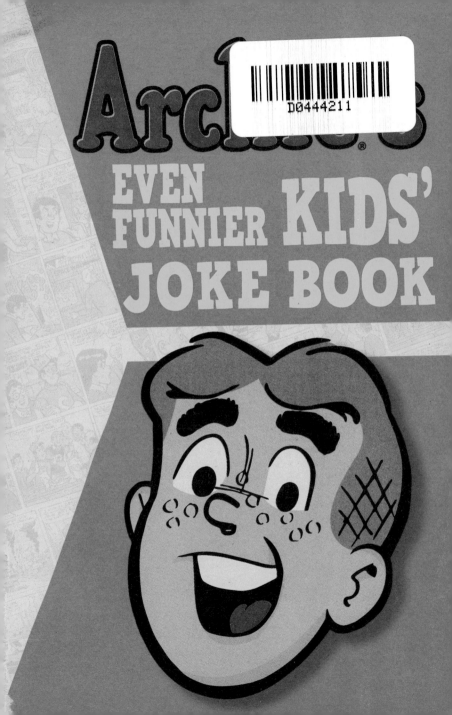

Archie's
EVEN FUNNIER KIDS'
JOKE BOOK

Archie's

EVEN FUNNIER KIDS' JOKE BOOK

Published by Archie Comic Publications, Inc.
325 Fayette Avenue, Mamaroneck, New York 10543-2318.

ArchieComics.com
ISBN: 978-1-936975-67-9

Publisher / Co-CEO: Jon Goldwater
Co-CEO: Nancy Silberkleit
President: Mike Pellerito
Co-President / Editor-In-Chief: Victor Gorelick
Senior Vice President - Sales / Business Development: Jim Sokolowski
Senior Vice President - Publishing / Operations: Harold Buchholz
Vice President - Special Projects: Steve Mooar
Executive Director of Editorial: Paul Kaminski
Director of Publicity & Marketing: Steven Scott
Project Coordinator & Book Design: Joe Morciglio
Production Manager: Stephen Oswald
Proofreader / Editorial Assistant: Carly Inglis
Production: Duncan McLachlan
Production Intern: Claudia Stoller, Jeff Miller

Archie's

YOU DID

EVEN FUNNIER KIDS' JOKE BOOK

LAUGHS AND GAGS BY:

BOB MONTANA, FRANK DOYLE,
BILL VIGODA, GEORGE GLADIR,
AL HARTLEY, BILL GOLLIHER
HY EISMAN, DICK MALMGREN
BOB BOLLING, SAMM SCHWARTZ
STAN GOLDBERG, DAN PARENT
FERNANDO RUIZ, HARRY LUCEY
DAN DECARLO JR., JEFF SHULTZ,
JOE EDWARDS, RUDY LAPICK,
RICH KOSLOWSKI, BOB SMITH
TERRY AUSTIN, BARRY GROSSMAN
TITO PENA, JOE MORCIGLIO
JON D'AGOSTINO, BILL YOSHIDA
JACK MORELLI, AND DAN DECARLO

…ID IT!

You've just picked up the ultimate book of funny panels, crazy cartoons, wacky jokes and terrible puns! If you didn't actually buy it, go and bug your parents until they do!

You'll find all sorts of crazy stuff in this book. From sports gags and food puns to wacky one-liners and riddles, the jokes just keep on coming!

So, what are you waiting for?

Go on! Get reading! GO!

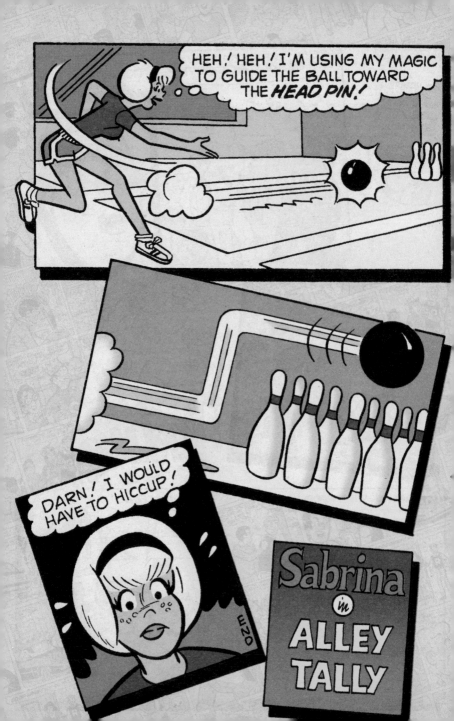

Q: WHAT IS BLACK, WHITE & RED ALL OVER?

A: A ZEBRA WITH A NOSEBLEED!

Q: WHAT DID THE RIB-EYE SAY TO THE PORTERHOUSE?

FACULTY FUNNIES™

CHAPTER 4

CHAPTER 5

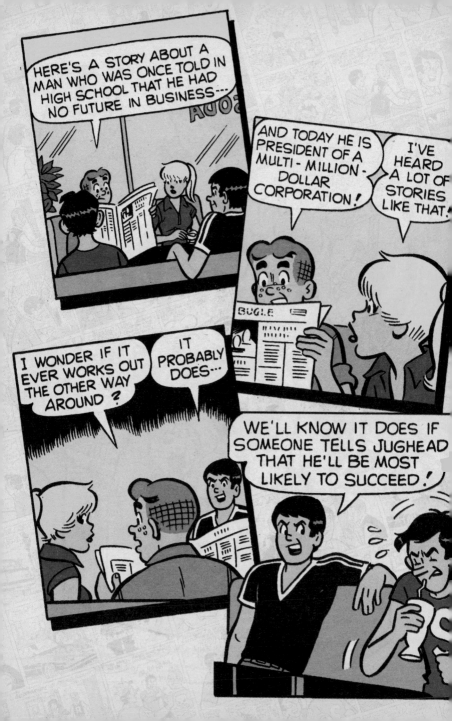

DIPSY DOODLES

END

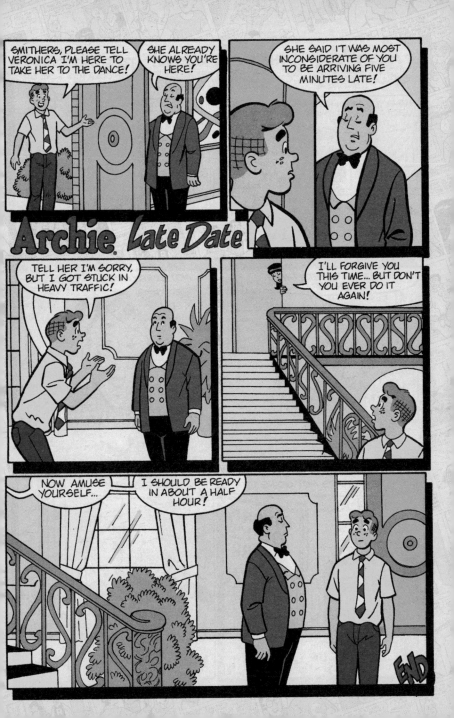

EASY DOES IT

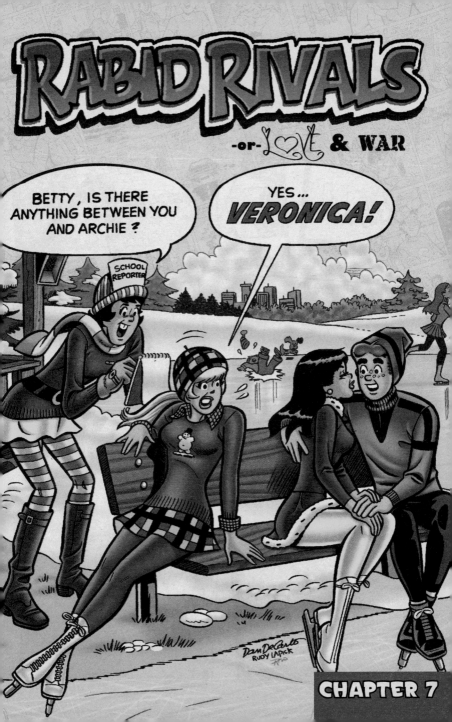

Jughead IN "THRIFT DRIFT"

Betty PINUP

Moose IN CHICK KICK

MISS BEAZLY'S GAG BAG

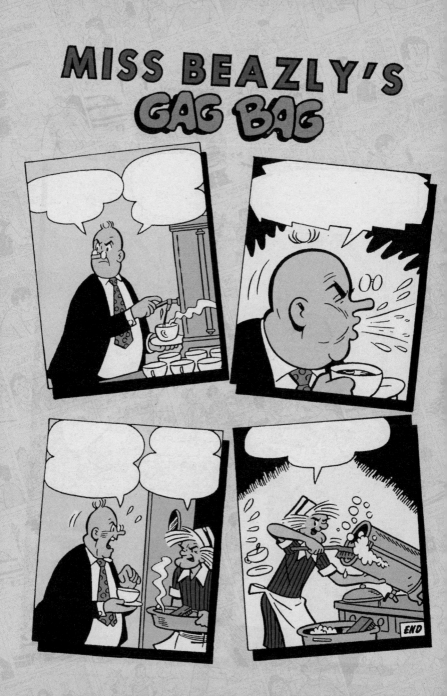

VERONICA'S PIN-UP